Res

*How To Write A Resume And Get The Job
Interview That You Want*

Contents

Introduction

I wish to thank you for choosing this book; I know you will find the content informative and helpful in your quest for your dream job. Whatever your current work status, one thing remains as important as ever, your resume.

With the information this book contains you will be able to produce a resume that will contain everything a prospective employer could be looking for, and also presented in the correct way.

Whatever profession you are hoping to join a good resume is your key to landing an interview and this book; *"Resume Writing – How To Write A Resume And Get The Job Interview That You Want"* covers the main topics in depth, all of which make up the ingredients for a killer resume. Having a good resume will get you an interview, which is technically a foot in the door to getting you that job.

Stop putting off writing or editing your resume, instead check out this book and get your resume right:

● Job hunting made easy with the right resume

● The benefits of a polished resume

● Resume formats

● Get started in the right way

- Resume content

- Using a template

- Online resume services

- Land the perfect job

- Be more employable

- Keep your dignity

I wish you luck and thank you again for choosing this book, I hope you find it helpful and wish you all the best on your search for the perfect job.

Chapter 1 – Job Hunting Made Easy With The Right Resume

No matter what your current work status or what you want to achieve, most people will need some kind of employment at some time during their life.

There are lots of things that can make finding the right employment easier; with the most important making yourself as employable as possible. A good indicator of how employable you are is your resume. Your resume provides a prospective employer with a first impression of you, and is definitely the best way to get your foot in the door. There are many other reasons why you want a good resume. A good resume will benefit you, even when you are not actively looking for employment.

Understanding the various benefits linked with resume writing can motivate you and make sure you get everything right from the beginning. Not only will you just be submitting your resume, this is also a great opportunity to show how employable and versatile you are.

When you begin to write your resume you need to keep the following points at the forefront of your mind:

1. There are different resume formats, each one can be submitted for various purposes. Choosing the right resume for your needs will really make a difference.

2. What will make your resume stand out in front of a prospective employer?

3. What will make the employer want to pick you over the other candidates?

Paying attention when you begin compiling your resume will give you the best chance of getting noticed. There are a number of factors that are associated with writing a resume and we will cover all of these in detail in further chapters, so that you can put together a resume that is perfectly tailored to your needs. The amount of information that you decide to include will differ from one circumstance to another. By ensuring that you look at all of the elements in advance you have a far better likelihood of writing a resume which is going to work for you.

One of the things that people struggle with when they start writing a resume is the fact that they have never written one before. If you are in this situation you may consider using a free template in order to get the basis for your own resume. Whilst there are benefits to using a template there are also disadvantages which are covered in a separate chapter.

Although it is very important to have a resume too successfully land a job there are other factors you need to consider. Timing everything properly will be paramount to landing the job, as will the way you conduct yourself. Play your cards right and the job will be yours and you will soon be going places. It is also necessary for you to make yourself as employable as possible and this is an element often overlooked. Currently we live in an age where it is relatively easy to find information about almost anyone with or without their knowledge. You may do some research on a potential employer and their company, but you can be sure that they will be doing research of their own on you!

There are a number of elements that are associated to finding the job of your dreams; however the first thing that you should consider is writing a proper resume. By doing so correctly you will find that you can land the employment that you want even in the current times when the job market is more volatile than ever.

Chapter 2 – The Benefits of a Polished Resume

If you were to ask any of your friends and acquaintances why they were writing a resume the answers will generally be the same and this is to secure a job. In reality landing the job is only one of the benefits that can be associated with writing a resume. There are a number of benefits that you will experience which are likely to follow you as you change employment through the years.

This chapter is going to cover some of the reasons why it is a great idea to write a resume, and why you should make the effort to focus on this incredibly important document.

The benefits of having a polished resume are not limited; however the most important are as follows:

Get Hired

Probably the most obvious benefit you will get from writing a great resume is that it will increase your chances of getting hired. This is the primary reason for writing your resume and by writing it properly you will increase the odds substantially of getting the job.

First Impression

Write your resume properly and you will leave a great first impression which the prospective employer will remember for some time. This first impression begins with you starting your resume properly and then capturing the attention of those who are reading it.

Skills

When you find that you are sitting in an interview it can be really difficult to outline your skills, as you will more than likely forget something or be unable to get the correct information across in the right manner, possibly due to nerves. Writing a proper resume means that you can highlight your skills in the best way possible and ensure that nothing gets forgotten.

Etiquette

Etiquette is one of the main reasons for making sure you write a well-developed, grammatically correct resume as it proves to the prospective employer that you are au fait with business etiquette. This is particularly important if you are applying for a post where you will be expected to practice business etiquette on a regular basis.

Communication

The likelihood of you ending up sitting in front of a prospective employer is very high with the right resume. When you find yourself in this scenario it can be difficult to maintain focus and convey all of the information that you want to. This could be due to nerves and no matter how many interviews you do, they are all going to be different. Submitting a well written resume that you have taken time preparing will show that you are able to communicate at any level and particularly with those in charge.

Value

Your resume is the perfect place to showcase what value you could bring to the company if you were hired. This is without a doubt one of the biggest benefits of a resume, it provides you with the opportunity to speak even before you actually open your mouth! This is the time to let the prospective employer know about any ongoing training that you are doing or have completed as well as any additional qualifications. Your resume does not only add value to you, but you can also add value to your resume.

Whilst these are just a few of the main benefits you can obtain when writing a detailed and well thought out resume, they can also help you to stay motivated in the exercise of crafting your resume, to ensure that it stands out from all of the resumes submitted by other candidates.

Chapter 3 – Resume Formats and What They Mean for You

There are unlimited ways in which you can write a resume however there are certain formats that should be amongst the ones that you consider. There are three main formats used when writing a resume and by following one of them you will know that you have used the correct resume etiquette.

There is nothing stopping you from deviating from these formats but it is very important that you choose the basic format that is right for your circumstances and needs. The following are the three ways in which you can write your resume:

Chronologically

This is probably the most common format used to write a resume and can be tailored for most circumstances. When choosing this format you must remember that the chronological entry of information needs to be written in reverse order, meaning that your most current information is at the top and then works down through your work and education history.

Using this format you need to follow chronological order for your work history and education and it is acceptable for you to go back 15 years, although you can include older history if it is relevant to the position that you are applying for or you feel it is necessary. It is your resume and as such it is your decision how much information you decide to include, however when you are working in a chronological format it is expected that your work and educational history will span for at least the previous 10 years.

Generally a chronological style format will work best if you have been in the same field for a number of years and you are not planning on moving from this type of profession in the near future. If your application is for a position that is similar to your current position the chronological format works equally as well.

Functional

Unlike the chronological format discussed above, when choosing to use a functional format you are going to focus more on your skills and what you can do in direct association with the work you are applying for. Doing this means that you can outline specific areas where you believe you will be a benefit to the company, either through your work experience or education.

Generally the functional format of a resume is used if you have worked in a variety of professions throughout your employment history. You do not want a prospective employer to be looking at employment that is completely unrelated to the position that you are applying for. Additionally if you have large gaps in your employment history it is better to choose the functional format.

Many people find themselves in a position where they are entering the workforce either directly from school or after they have been out of the workplace for a number of years. In both of these cases you will find that a functional format for your resume will work better than a chronological format as it allows you to focus on what you are able to do rather than your history which could either have gaps or be nonexistent.

Hybrid

There could be times when you want to combine the benefits offered by both the chronological and functional formats, and when you choose this format it is known as the hybrid format. When using a hybrid format you do not need to mix everything, you may decide to focus on one particular area such as your education or work history and craft the information in such a way that you look far more attractive to the perspective employer.

Generally those who choose to use the hybrid format are normally looking to change direction and get into a new field of work or make a dramatic career change. The hybrid format is beneficial in these circumstances because it allows you, the writer to have the opportunity to highlight your skills and level of experience. The hybrid format is also an excellent way to highlight something specific within your resume, but you do not want to completely step away from the chronological format.

Chapter 4 – Get Started in the Right Way

What is the first thing that you typically do when you meet someone for the first time? No doubt you will be similar to the vast majority of people and start by exchanging greetings prior to introducing yourself. Giving someone your resume is no different; the resume essentially introduces you as an individual to the place of employment. It is for this reason that you need to pay particular attention to the heading of your resume, because this is where your information starts. Making sure that you format the information properly shows immediately that you are serious about employment, as well as making things easy and convenient for the prospective employer.

The heading of your resume should be on the top of your very first page, generally there is no need to include a title page with your resume unless you are applying for a very specific job. You need to keep your resume short and to the point; this is one of the best ways to guarantee that you will be noticed. If it is possible for you to fit all of the relevant information onto a single page, the perspective employer will certainly appreciate the effort. However, you need to make sure that your resume is still legible and easy to read. If you choose to use a tiny font the only place your resume will end up is in the bin as it will be difficult to read. If you are writing your resume using Microsoft Word, you should not use the header feature; just begin at the top of the page. The information that you should include in this area is specific and whilst this may sound basic it is paramount that you get this right and review it properly. The information that should be included in your heading will be as follows:

Name

Your name should be at the very top of the page. If an interviewer is looking through a number of resumes to find a specific one it is important that your resume stands out. To ensure that this is the case, put your name in bold at the top of the page. There is no need to use a different font, underline or italicize your name, making it bold is enough to ensure that it stands out.

Address

It is important to include your address so that you can be contacted if necessary. Although it may be convenient to use a post office box this is not an appropriate practice on a resume. Using a post office box could make the prospective employer view you as no more than a temporary prospect. The only time it would be acceptable to use a post office box is if you are planning to move to a new address. Using your street address displays more stability and is the preferred resume etiquette.

Phone Number

Your phone number is really important and whilst you may have multiple phone numbers just choose one. This should be your primary number, the one that you will answer when it is called. Remember to check your voicemail on your phone and be sure that any answer phone message you have is professional providing clear information that indicates the caller has dialed the right number. Do not use amusing messages, also do not have a standard message which simply states the phone number as this can put people off of leaving a message.

Internet

It is important that you also include some internet contact information on your resume; this includes your primary email address, website if you have one and also your LinkedIn account. Prospective employers may prefer to contact you this way.

Additional Headings

The primary heading goes on the top of the first page, however if your resume spans more than one page it will be beneficial for you to also include a short heading at the top of any additional pages. Include basic information here, such as your name, phone number and email address. This way if the pages of your resume somehow get separated it makes it far easier to allocate them correctly.

First impressions count, you get one chance to make an impression and this is why it is so important that the first thing seen is a bold heading which is formatted correctly.

Chapter 5 – Resume Content

When it comes to the content for your resume you have a number of elements that you can include. There is no set criterion of what you should and should not include and this chapter will focus solely on what you can include in your resume content, along with the reasons why you might choose to include certain elements.

Is a Job Objective Statement Necessary?

Usually you will want to provide information in your resume that informs the prospective employer of the position you are applying for. On a traditional resume this information would form part of a job objective statement, and this is something you can include in any type of resume provided it is used properly. There are several other elements which may prove more beneficial to you and will depend on your needs and the circumstances of the position you are applying for.

The following outlines the reasons why you should or should not include a job objective statement. If you choose to go with a typical job objective statement it will be placed near to the top of your resume. Although it is not necessary to place it here and if it is obvious which position you are applying for the statement is actually redundant and unnecessary.

If you are applying for work that is significantly different to anything that you have done in the past or if you are applying for a very specific job, using a job objective statement could be the best choice and it helps to remove any confusion and it will streamline the whole process.

If you decide that using a job objective statement is the best way forward it is important that it is formatted properly. This way the information will be easier for the employer to find, it will saves them time and this is something they will really appreciate. The first thing that you need to include in this statement is the position you are applying for. Make sure that you are very specific about the position you are applying for particularly if the company has more than one job vacancy available. As well as being specific about the role, include information about any responsibilities that are associated with the job. Finally you need to include information to guide the reader through your resume and confirms that the information contained in the resume has direct relation to the job you are applying for.

More important than including specific information on your job objective statement is the way in which you word it. It is important that you do not use too many words otherwise any benefit will be lost in the context. Your job objective statement should be no more than two lines.

If you decide not to include a job objective statement, you can still be professional and specific about the job you are applying for by using a professional title, as this will allow the prospective employer to see who you are and what you can offer.

Employers can determine where you would best fit into their company as soon as they read this brief description.

Qualifications

When you write your resume always keep in mind that the person reading it will more than likely have stacks of resumes to get through, and it can be a very cumbersome task to read every detail before they make the decision on which candidates they are going to call. This is why it is advisable to have a brief summary outlining your qualifications and then additional information that you feel would be beneficial for the actual interviewer. You can place the qualification summary in a section of its own with a heading alerting the interviewer to the fact that you are providing a summary. This summary should ideally be near to the top of the first page, under your heading or in the job objective statement if you are using one. Bold the heading so that your summary stands out and be sure to only include information that is necessary as your aim should be to provide the interviewer with your qualifications and why they should take a closer look at your resume.

Remember that you have other sections in your resume where you can outline your qualifications and levels of experience in more detail. For example you may choose to have a section for any education that is relevant and specific to the job you are applying for, you may also have a work history listed. This information will be detailed therefore it is not necessary to include it all in the summary of your qualifications. The shorter and more concise you are the easier it will be for the interviewer to see what you have to offer.

The length of your summary is not dictated, however it is a good idea to keep this short, a brief paragraph about your qualifications is all you need. Be sure to write this paragraph in a way that speaks to the reader and is not just a list of facts.

Experience
When it comes to writing your experience make sure this is tailored to the position you are trying to secure and that it is directly related. This is one of the sections that you may find it necessary to change every time you apply for a different position.

Background
Only include background information about you and or your work history, again this should be specific to the position you are applying for.

Ethics

When you apply for a job the interviewer will not only want to know about your education and work history, they will also want to gauge you as a person and find out something about you. More often than not this will directly relate to the ethics that are part of the company's practice.

Values

You should include information relating to your personal values, but it is important to make sure these are relevant to the position you are applying for.

When writing any of these sections, particularly the qualifications section, it is important that you blow your own trumpet without appearing arrogant. Do not be afraid to tell the employer what you can do to enhance the position and how you will fit in as a team player. This is the best place to name drop (if you can) as at times it's not what you know, it's who you know.

Your resume is an advert that promotes you and as so you want it to speak to the reader in the way that proves to them you are the right candidate for the job. There will be times when the summary of qualifications will be the only section of your resume that is read and as so you need to shine in this element if you want a chance of progressing to the interview stage.

When collating your resume do not make claims that you are unable to substantiate. It is really important to speak highly of yourself and your qualifications, but you need to be able to back everything up. If your qualification summary is so good you get noticed you want to make sure that you are being noticed for the right reasons and not purely for your unique writing prowess!

Outline Your Experience

So far we have covered some of the different sections to include in your resume, but these really only make up who you are and your capabilities. Now you need to look at the longer sections which you need to include in your resume as these will also be of interest to a prospective employer. An outline of your experience will be of particular interest so you need to make sure that you give this section the attention it deserves. This section will be looked at thoroughly by any interviewer and is also the chance for you to make sure you have covered the things that you may forget at interview.

Now we need to look at things you need to include as well as how you can overcome any difficulties that may exist. Begin by considering the format you have chosen to use and making sure that you have completed the format using the correct protocol. If you have chosen the chronological format means that you need to make sure that you have the information in the correct order. If you opt for the functional format you must begin with any work experience you have which is directly related to the job you are applying for. This should be followed by your employment history placed in order with regards to the level of experience you have which is associated and relevant to the position you are applying for. Finally if you have chosen a hybrid format, then you can use either chronological or functional formats and tailor these to suit your exact requirements.

Your aim should be to include enough information so an interviewer can see at a glance both your experience and job history. The basic information you need to include is your job title, name of the employer and the employers address. You can also include specific information about what you have achieved in your previous positions. Keep this information concise, too much detail will lead to a cluttered resume full of unnecessary information. Aim to add three bullet points under each job, as this should provide a good overview. Be concise when you describe the basic information about previous employment, do not get bogged down on details, the year that you worked somewhere will be enough, there is no need for a date or month.

It would be great if everyone had a perfect work history, however this is not usually the case. There are many reasons why people may have gaps in their employment or information they would rather not disclose. The following are the most common problems that can occur with regards to employment history and the ways in which these can be overcome.

If you have been in the same employment for years, this could be a perfect opportunity for you to be discriminated against due to your age; just another reason for limiting your work history. When working in chronological format you should start with the most recent job and never go back further than 15 years. Making the mistake of listing every job you have ever had could lead to age related questions. The only reason for you to do this is if you use the functional format and need to include experience gained from more than 15 years ago.

Another issue which relates to gaps in employment is where someone has less desirable circumstances. For example they could have left a previous position in less than favourable circumstances or maybe been laid off for an extended period, or simply chose to take a break from employment. The best way to make sure that any gaps do not trigger unnecessary questions is to assign a title to whatever you may have been doing whilst you were technically unemployed. This time may not have been paid employment but the chances are you can find a plausible name to assign to this period/s. Be honest when doing this, there is no set rules that you have to be employed by an outside employer, after all during this time you have still been building experience.

Celebrate Your Successes

When you are ready to compile this part of your resume, you will have started properly and included the basic information including your work history and education. These elements will be looked at very carefully by a prospective interviewer and therefore need to include details. It is likely that you may have additional information you want to include on your resume but does not necessarily fit into these sections. If this is the case you need to find a way to list these achievements in a way that is beneficial to you and will make it easier for you to land that dream job.

It is important all of your achievements are recognized, and these will be of interest to any potential employer. The aim of your resume is to make yourself as employable as possible and the best way for you to do this is by ensuring that the interviewer is provided with everything that you have to offer. This should include personal and professional achievements, particularly if they relate in any way to the position you are applying for.

You may find it beneficial to break up your personal and professional achievements so that the interviewer can look through both or either one easily. If you feel that you have specific achievements and want to ensure these are noticed because you feel they have direct relevance to the position, write your resume in functional format and you can then add your achievements to the same section.

There are a number of different elements you can include to make up your achievement section, the most common are as follows:

1. Unpaid Work

The majority of your resume will relate to work completed during normal working hours, however you may be really proud of what you do during your personal time. You may partake in various types of community services or other type of unpaid work. What you do during this time will not only be considered with regards to experience, this information is also a great moral reflection of your character too.

2. Awards

You should list any awards that you have received regardless of whether these are personal or professional. Any awards will indicate your moral character or your business ethics both of which will be highly desirable to prospective employers. Winning awards are also a good way to demonstrate what a good team player you are, this is another attribute that many employers look for.

3. Affiliations

Many people are associated with organizations directly related to their profession. If you have any professional

affiliations these should be included on your resume
either in order of importance or alphabetically.

4. Skills

You may have skills a prospective employer would find
interesting, but they will never know unless you tell
them. For example you may be extremely technical, able
to work your way around a computer with little effort.
This is a skill that would be of interest in almost any
position you may apply for. Include any relevant skills or
interest that you have, also remember that if you can
speak any foreign languages these are also desirable in
the workplace.

4. Publications

If you have any type of publications including research
papers, books or articles you have personally written or
taken part in, be sure to include this information.

5. Personal Interests

Whilst this is something that typically goes at the end of
the achievement section of your resume, it is always
good to include your personal interests. Whether they
are related to the position you are applying for or not
there could be something that may seem irrelevant to
you that the employer finds most desirable.

These are just a few of the different elements that you
should consider adding in your achievement section. The
idea is for you to make sure you include everything that

shows you are a qualified candidate for the job. Make sure that you are not overly personal and do not go into too much detail, just provide an overview of you and what you can offer and you won't go wrong.

Education

Depending on the position you are applying for you may need to focus on your education. There are times when this could be the first thing a prospective employer will look at, particularly if they are looking for a specific degree or particular certificate which is associated with your education. With this in mind it is important that you know how to make your education stand out and also how it can be set out to your best advantage.

Very few people will ever have an education which is specific to the job they are applying for. You could be awaiting results of your higher education or degree; or maybe you are still attending classes. These are specific circumstances and need to be considered carefully when applying for a job as well as completing your resume. By making sure that you put everything down on paper properly, means that you will look good on paper and help you to get you a seat in front of the interviewer.

The section involving your education will be at the end or very near the end of your resume. There are some reasons that could make you consider placing this information nearer the front of your resume. The following are all good reasons why you may choose to place your educational section nearer the front:

You are a recent graduate – if you have recently received your degree or you are working with a recently awarded high school diploma, it will be far better for you to include this information earlier in your resume. This information will be of particular interest to the interviewer especially if you have the right education for the job but lack experience.

Relevant education – your education will either be really relevant to the job you are applying for or have no relevance at all. Either way it is wise to include this early on in your resume, particularly if the education is specific to the job because this will prove that you are a more qualified candidate for the position. There is no shame with making yourself look as employable as possible and including any relevant education is a great way to do this.

Degree but no experience – having a degree that is specific to the job but no experience could be seen as an issue and may be problematical. This is usual for recent graduates and also applies to those who may have graduated but gone directly into another field. If you have the education that is relevant but no experience, disclose this early in your resume.

With your education be as detailed as possible; include the college you attended, the classes and the number of credits gained. You should include classes that you have attended even if they did not lead to a degree, or in cases where you may or may not be planning to go back and finish your degree in the future. If you are currently attending classes be sure to specify this information on your resume and the date you are expecting to graduate.

List all of your certificates on your resume in the educational section. There are some jobs where a professional certificate will mean more to the employer than a college degree. This is why it is very important for you to make sure you remember to list everything.

Chapter 6 – Should You Use a Template?

The task of writing a resume from scratch can be really daunting and there are a lot of people that struggle to get all of the relevant information down even when using a general guide. When you reach this point you may consider using a template to design your resume so that you can create something quickly and easily.

There are many benefits to using a template; however there are also some potential problems and this is why you need to understand the problems so that you can avoid them.

Templates can be most beneficial; firstly they can help you to get started with the process of writing and formatting of your resume. Although a template will not put down any information specific to your educational work experience it will be able to assist by providing an overview of what information needs to be included and where this should be placed. Finding yourself staring at a blank page and not knowing where to go will lead to procrastination, simply because you have no idea where you should start. Using a template will get you past this point, however you should only use the template as a general guide.

Amongst the downsides of a template is that there are thousands of potential templates for you to choose from. Many will not provide you with the information and are also not provided in a format that is acceptable. For example you may choose a standard resume template through Microsoft Word or an alternative word program. These templates will be beneficial to give you some general guidance but you need to be cautious about the specifics that they offer. These types of templates may put your name at the top of the resume in large, bold letters and whilst it is important to get your name noticed, it is what you put under your name that is vitally important, as this includes your contact information such as email address and telephone number.

Many resume templates will provide this information in fine print which is difficult to read especially to someone who has to read through a number of resumes one after the other. This is just one of the reasons that you will have to edit the template to a certain extent; you should be perfecting the resume in accordance with your own requirements and not seeing the template as an authority on resume creation. You should be cautious about the limited amount of information which may be included in a resume template. Your resume is a way for you to market yourself; therefore you need to put down enough information so you are marketing yourself effectively.

The resume template may include general information with regards to where you should place your work history or educational achievements. The template is unlikely to provide you with the information that you require for your personal achievements and summary, and these are both elements that you should be intending to use to catch the attention of the interviewer. Another reason to be cautious when using a template is that it can be obvious that you have used this short cut. The last thing you want to do is to portray yourself as lazy or not committed with regards to your job application. Taking a short cut including the use of a standard resume template may make it difficult for you to get past the initial selection process. Another disadvantage with using a standard template could be that several others may have used the same template resulting in a lot of applications looking very similar; your aim is to stand out not blend in to the crowd.

Templates can be beneficial but only if you use them in a general sense, and even if you do decide to use a template you should still format everything rather than sticking with the standard formatting and include additional information that markets you properly.

By all means use a template if you really feel that it is necessary, just make sure you modify it in order to present yourself as the professional that you are.

Chapter 7 – Online Resume Services

Although the majority of people see a resume as a written document that is printed and handed in when applying for a job, there are many additional benefits to also having an online resume.

Most companies now use the Internet exclusively, and may request that you send them an online application rather than submitting something printed. To do this you need to know how to effectively format your resume so that it is acceptable for electronic distribution.

There are some specific differences between an online resume and a printed resume. The primary difference is that one is usually written in Microsoft Word or other type of word processor and then formatted to fit on to a printed page. An electronic resume must be collated in a different format for easy online distribution. The following are some of the most common resume formats you may want to consider regarding electronic resumes.

PDF

You should always convert your resume to a PDF and most word processors have the ability to do this automatically. You can also download a program relatively easily so that your resume will also print in PDF form. The primary benefit of using a PDF is that this is a universal document which can be viewed on any operating system. A PDF document can also be formatted so that the data is compressed making it easier to send via email.

Microsoft Word

It might be necessary for you to have your resume in Microsoft word and this is the format that most employers will request. You are more likely to have used this program or something very similar to write your resume, so there is not too much trouble to send your resume in this format. When using this program you have to pay particular attention to the formatting as a prospective employer should be able to open a Microsoft word document even if they use a newer form of this program such as .docx. Just remember to save your resume in Microsoft word format.

Plain Text

There may be times when it is necessary for you to have your resume in a plain text format. It is unlikely that you will have to distribute your resume in this format to a prospective employer but this may be necessary if you are wanting to copy and paste sections into online forums or specific resume services.

Email

If you know that you are going to be regularly emailing your resume you can do this either in PDF format or you can format the email so that most email recipients can read it clearly.

HTML

It might be necessary for you to produce your resume in an HTML file and then upload onto an online service. The benefit of using HTML is that you can format the document in any way you need too and this includes changing the font, color, spacing etc. You may find that it takes time to format this document but there are a number of online services that offer free HTML tools, making it easy to achieve the same end result.

Subject Line and Keywords

Another important thing for you to remember is to consider the subject line and keywords that will be associated with your online resume. This is particularly true if you are frequently emailing your resume or if you put your resume online for more exposure.

The subject line should be concise so the recipient knows exactly what you are sending. If you get too creative with the subject line in a hope that the recipient will open the email quicker, this is more likely to annoy the recipient and could be why you miss out on the opportunity to interview.

There could also be possibilities where you could passively search for jobs online, and to do so you need to choose the proper keywords to include in your online resume. When local employers are looking for perspective employees they are likely to conduct a search on the internet using industry keywords. Making sure that you have included these words in your resume will make you far more likely to be found. You do not need to overdo the keywords but should consciously make sure that some are included in your resume.

Chapter 8 – Land The Perfect Job

One of the most important factors when it comes to landing the right job is definitely your resume. There are other factors that will be considered during the interview process and beyond; therefore this chapter has been designed to discuss these elements further as you need to focus on the entire package and not just posting the perfect resume.

The following things are what the majority of interviewers look for and will be impressed when you provide and execute them well.

Dress and Grooming

When attending an interview make sure that you dress appropriately, whilst there is no need to dress up to the nines you should dress in a way that will get you noticed, just not for the wrong reasons. Aim for one level above the standard for the company where the interview will be taking place.

Be Prepared

One of the most common mistakes that people make when attending an interview is that they are not prepared. You should research the company you are attending and if possible research the person conducting the interview. There is no need to use this information but having some background information on the company will help to get the interview moving along nicely.

Timing

The last thing you want to do when attending an interview is to turn up late. There may be a time where you are late due to circumstances that are completely beyond your control, such as a flat tire. Make every effort to be early for your interview and if you are going to be late, contact the company and let them know well in advance.

Extra Copies

Always carry extra copies of your resume when you attend an interview just in case the company does not have your copy to hand or there is more than one person interviewing. More often you will not need the copies but it will certainly impress an interviewer if you hand them a fresh copy of your resume when they need it.

Body Language

Whilst it is not necessary for you to become a body language expert you should avoid any problems that the interviewer could be watching for. Particular problems that occur are looking at the floor, fidgeting, tapping your foot or shaking your leg. Be sure to initiate eye contact, hold your head up high and keep your feet flat on the floor!

Relax

Interviews are nerve wracking, particular when it is you sat in the hot seat; however there is no reason for you to be so wound up that you end up blowing your chance. Relax as much as you can (without slouching!) and speak clearly and naturally. Adopt a friendly tone without being overly familiar with the interviewer.

List

Although you are going to be the one asked the questions, there is no reason why you cannot ask questions of your own. Asking questions shows that you are interested and have really considered the position. Questions about the company, position etc. will all be received well. Be sure to write down your questions and take these with you to the interview to ensure that you don't forget them through nerves.

Follow up

Another important thing which is often overlooked is the way in which you can follow up your interview. It would be beneficial to immediately follow up your interview with an email that is short and to the point, thank the interviewer for their time and let them know that you look forward to hearing from them. You can also send a hand written card through UPS which is a nice touch. If you hear nothing within a week then email once more so they know you are still interested and include a brief overview of your qualifications and why you think you are the perfect candidate for the job.

Chapter 9 – Be More Employable

Following on from the things that you can do when you get the interview and also straight after to successfully land the job there are many other things you need to consider and when you have considered these carefully you will see that they will make a big difference in you being employable or missing out on your perfect job.

It is possible to research almost everything and anything online and this includes you. It is important that you believe any potential interviewer will have researched you in advance, they will have been looking for any information that provides them with an insight in to your moral character. Unfortunately many people have found themselves in a difficult situation due to posts that were made on Facebook or other social media networks. You may have thought it was funny to post a picture of you messing about and having a good night out, however this could prove to be a huge red flag when it comes to landing your dream job.

Prior to applying and submitting your resume for a job, make sure that you have done your best to clean up your social media accounts. Remove posts and pictures that may portray you in a bad way and this should be done as soon as you can. There may be cases where this will prove to be a difficult process particularly if the pictures were posted on the wrong social media network.

You should also be concerned about things your friends may have posted about you. Depending on the job that you are trying to get and the ability of the interviewer this information will be relatively easy for them to find. Contact your friends that may have these things posted and ask them to remove the content as soon as possible. Explain why this is so important to you and that it could be the difference between securing or losing your dream job.

Research your own name on Google as you may be surprised at the information this may throw up about you. It could be that there is an image on Google images that portrays you in a bad light and this could even be from years ago. Take the time and effort to clean up this part of your history because the chances are that you will be researched in exactly this way.

Keeping your online reputation clean is one of the best ways that you can make yourself instantly more employable. This and having written a winning resume, arriving punctually and interviewing well and you will be quite surprised at how easy it can be to secure your dream job, particularly when you have taken the time and trouble to connect all of the dots.

Chapter 10 – Keep Your Dignity

Now that you have all of the relevant information that you need to successfully apply for your dream job and you know how to submit a perfect resume. There is just one last thing to consider and this will be when you land the dream job, how you leave your current place of employment.

You have two options, either you leave with your dignity or take out all of your frustrations and leave under a cloud of fury. It is really important that you maintain your dignity for one specific reason. There will be times when you have been badly treated in your current work place and you may be completely justified in thinking that you should voice your opinion and let everyone know exactly what you think of them. However, by doing this technically you are burning your bridges and when you burn your bridges there will be no chance of you ever returning.

Even when you feel that you will never want or need to return your actions can return and haunt you at some point in the future. There is a chance that you may need to contact this employer for a reference or even for employment in an emergency. Either way if you burn your bridges all you are doing is limiting your opportunities.

Be happy that you were able to land your dream job by writing a killer resume and interviewing well. You will find that when you put some distance between you and your previous employment it will all soon fade into the background, this also allows you to focus solely on the new employment that you have worked so hard to secure.

Conclusion

Now that you have come to the end of "Resume Writing - How to write a resume and get the job interview that you want" I do hope that you have found it to be informative and useful as you start taking your first steps towards getting an interview for your dream job.

All that is left is for you to use all of this information and make any necessary changes, re write or edit your resume and begin applying to the job that you really yearn for.

Good luck and thanks again for choosing this book

Made in the USA
Las Vegas, NV
12 August 2023

75991283R00031